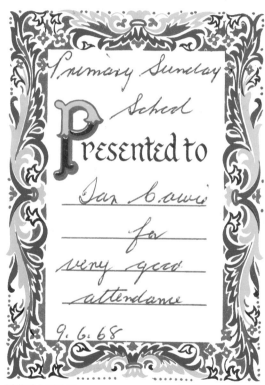

Primary Sunday School

Presented to

Ian C. awie

for

very good

attendance

9. 6. 68

PICKERING & INGLIS LTD.   PRINTED IN GREAT BRITAIN

The Boy with the Loaves and Fishes

Jesus and the others made their way up the quiet hillside.

(p. 35)

The Boy with the Loaves and Fishes

Enid Blyton

Illustrated by
ELSIE WALKER

LUTTERWORTH PRESS

LONDON

New Edition 1955
Second Impression 1956
Third Impression 1957
Fourth Impression 1959
Fifth Impression 1961
Sixth Impression 1963
Seventh Impression 1966

Printed in Great Britain by
William Clowes and Sons, Limited, London and Beccles

FOREWORD

At first, when Jesus rode into the city, nearly everyone was glad to see him, and they gave him a great welcome.

Later, many of them went back to their work and their homes and forgot about him. Some of them would have liked to stay, but when they heard that the rulers were against him they turned against him too. Others were disappointed because they expected Jesus to put the world right in a few minutes. When he did not give them what they wanted, they started looking for a new leader.

In the end, everyone left him—except the children. He was their hero and their friend. They did not understand everything about him, but they knew they could trust him, and they did not care what other people thought. They went on cheering and cheering and, when the rulers came to complain of the noise, they cheered louder still.

To-day many people have forgotten about Jesus

or turned away from him to other leaders, but he is still the most real person in the world.

The story that follows is the first of two stories of Jesus which Enid Blyton has written for you. We asked her to write them because she is the best story-teller we know about.

GORDON HEWITT

CONTENTS

SIMON HEARS A TALE

"I do want to go fishing," said Simon to himself, as he stood outside the door of his little white house up in the hills. "I know a fine place. I could catch plenty of fish for Mother."

It was early in the morning. The sun was coming over the hills, and Simon could feel its warmth all down his body to his bare toes. It was springtime and the grass on the hillside was bright with hundreds of flowers. Simon wanted to gather up his robe and go leaping down the green hill like one of his father's goats.

"Look at the Lake of Galilee far down

"I wonder if that wonderful man is in Capernaum to-day."

below, as blue as the sky!" said Simon. "That's where I want to go. Plenty of fish there for Mother. I could go and find my uncle and ask him to let me go out in his boat with him. If only Mother would let me."

A voice called from inside the cottage. "Simon! Where are you? Take your little sister for a few minutes while I get a meal for you all."

"Mother, it's a lovely day!" called back Simon. "Come and look. You can hardly see the town of Capernaum at the other end of the lake to-day—it's all hazy with sunshine."

His mother came out carrying Simon's little sister, a dark curly-haired child, only just awake. They stood there on the quiet hillside and looked down at the shimmering blue lake. They saw the little farmhouses here and there in the distance, built on the slope of the hills. They saw one or two boats on the lake.

"Yes, it's a lovely day," said Simon's mother. She looked towards the town of Capernaum, half-hidden in the blue distance. "I wonder if that wonderful man everyone is talking about is in Capernaum to-day."

"What wonderful man?" asked Simon. "Why is he wonderful?"

THE BOY WITH THE LOAVES AND FISHES

"He can make ill people well by just touching them with his hands," said his mother. "Your aunt Rachel was telling me about him yesterday. She was in Capernaum once when he was there, but the crowd was so great that she couldn't even get near enough to see him."

"What is his name?" asked Simon.

"Jesus," said his mother. "You would love to be with him, Simon, for he can tell all kinds of stories. Once he begins, you have to listen to the end."

"I wish I could hear him," said Simon. "You know how much I love stories, Mother. Tell me one he told."

"Oh, I'm no good at telling stories," said his mother. "I can't remember any that your aunt said Jesus told. Now come along and look after your sister for me."

"Mother, I want to go down to Capernaum and see this man," said Simon. "Let me go to-day."

"Now don't be foolish, Simon," said his mother. "You can't go alone all that way. It's too far. Besides, your father is going to take you to the farm with him, and you are to help him there. His master has said that he could do with a boy sometimes."

Simon thought it would be fun to go with his father. But he still wanted to go and find this wonderful man and see for himself what he did.

"Can I go with my father another day?" he asked. "I thought it would be good to go with my uncle, Mother, and sail out in his boat to help him with the fishing. He might put in at Capernaum then, and I could look for this man."

"No, Simon. You can't go fishing, and you can't go to Capernaum," said his mother. "You are to go with your father. But if you have been good all day, then perhaps I will let you go fishing with James this evening—just down to the lake and back for an hour."

Simon was disappointed. But still, it was better than nothing—James was his friend, and the two boys knew of a little hidden place by the lake-side where they sometimes caught fish. He would go there that evening, and perhaps he would bring home dozens of fine fish for his mother. Then she would pickle

The children sat outside in the sun

them and they could eat them with their
bread.

He took his little sister and played
with her while his mother got a meal
for his father. She called Simon. "Come
and get your loaves," she said. "There
are two for you and one for your sister."

Simon ran indoors. His mother held
out three loaves—but they were not the
kind we have: they were like flat thick
slices of bread—two for Simon, and one
for Ruth, his sister. The children sat outside in the sun, munching hungrily.

"One day," said Simon, pointing
down to the lake, "one day, Ruth, I
am going to have a big boat and I'm
going to sail out on the water down
there. If you're good, I might . . ."

Simon set off with his father

"Have you finished, Simon?" asked his father, coming out of the door. "Come along, then. You and your big boat! You work well to-day, my boy, and you can go fishing with James this evening. But there'll be no big boat and wide fishing-nets for you—you'll have to be content with your bare hands!"

Simon sprang up. He called good-bye to his mother and set off with his father, proud to be going to work with him. The sun was higher now. The lake was even bluer. More fishing-boats were out.

They went quickly down the grassy hill, and Simon tried to take as big strides as his father. "I shall work hard to-day," he thought. "I shall show my father I can work as well as a man."

SMALL FISHES

Simon did work hard that day. His father was pleased with him, and praised him. When they walked home together, he gave Simon a proud pat on the back.

"You did well, son," he said. "You hoed without shirking, and you mended that broken fence strongly. You're a good lad!"

Simon felt proud. He was very tired, but he was not going to show it. He kept up with his father. He was hungry too, and wished it was not such a long, uphill way home.

Behind the hills was a mountain, rising

much more steeply. Simon was glad his home was not up there! He had never been up that mountain, but he meant to one day. Then he gazed behind him, down at the lake.

Simon did work hard that day

It looked lovely. Simon thought how cool the water would be to his tired feet. When he had had a meal perhaps his mother would let him go fishing as she had said. He could call for James on his way.

"He's been a good lad," his father said, when they reached home. "We'll have a meal—and then Simon can have a rest. He must be tired."

"I don't want a rest," said Simon. "Can't I go fishing with James? You said I could, Mother. Do let me. It will be lovely down by the lake this evening. I'll bring you back plenty of fish for to-morrow!"

"Eat your supper first and then see if you still want to go," said his mother, and she gave him some bread and pickles. "You might like to play with Ruth. She has been lonely without you all day."

But after he had eaten his meal Simon wanted to go fishing. His mother gave him a little basket. "I hope it will be big enough to hold all the fish!" she said.

Simon set off across the slope of the green hill. The sun was sinking now, but there was still time to go down to the lake and back. He soon came to James's little white-washed house and called loudly.

"James! Come out and fish! Where do you think I've been all day? I've been working at the farm with my father."

James appeared at once. "Have you

really?" he said. "Mother, can I go with Simon?"

"Well, it's growing late," said his mother. "Don't be too long."

The boys darted down the hillside to the lake. They chose the steepest path, because then their legs seemed to go by themselves. They spread out their coats for the wind to catch, and yelled with joy to feel themselves going so fast.

Simon set off

"Now—let's be quiet," panted Simon as they came to the lake-side. "We don't want to frighten the fish."

It was a tiny inlet of water they had now come to, with bushes hanging over the water. The inlet was deep and quite big fish sometimes came into it.

The boys lay down flat, as quietly as they could. Simon nudged James. A big fish was swimming slowly below them.

They had no nets, only their bare hands. As quick as a cat James slid his hand into the water and grabbed at the fish. But it was away at once with a flick of its tail. Other fish came swimming by. Patiently the boys lay beside the water, their arms dangling in it, wet and cool, waiting to catch any unwary fish.

James caught two big ones and was delighted. He was quicker than Simon. Then Simon caught one, and was so surprised that he almost let it go.

"It's only a small one," he said, as he put it into his basket. "Not nearly as big as yours, James."

James caught another. He was pleased. "You can have one of mine," he said.

"No, you keep yours," said Simon. "Wait—here comes one!"

He pounced on the silvery fish—and held it! It was slippery and Simon was afraid it would get away. But soon it was safely in his basket. Now he had two—rather small ones, but still perhaps they would be big enough for his mother to pickle.

"We ought to go home," said James. "We'll have to hurry."

The two boys left the lake-side and made their way up the hill, talking. "Have you heard about that man called Jesus?" asked James.

"Yes," said Simon. "I wanted to go down to Capernaum and hear him telling stories and see him making ill people well—but Mother wouldn't let me."

"Did you know he could cure even mad people?" said James. "Well, he can. My father said so. And there's something more than that too—this man Jesus has brought dead people back to life again."

Simon stared at James, hardly believing him. Then he thought of something. "Do you remember when our donkey died last year?" he said. "Could he—could Jesus have made him come alive again? Mother cried. I did, too, because our donkey was my friend."

"He can do anything," said James. "He's a good man, and people say it's because he's so good and kind that he can do these things. I wish we could see him."

"I wouldn't dare to speak to him," said Simon. "I should be afraid. Look—there's your mother calling for you!"

The boys parted and Simon went to his own home.

"I was just beginning to worry about you," said his mother. "Have you caught me enough fish for to-morrow's meals?"

His father looked into Simon's basket and laughed.

"Fish! Look what he's caught—you can hardly see them. They're not worth pickling."

"Aren't they?" said Simon in a disappointed voice. His mother smiled at him.

"They're nice little fish," she said. "I shall certainly pickle them for you, Simon. You can eat them yourself with your bread to-morrow."

"Yes, I will," said Simon. "And next time I'll catch fish big enough for you, Mother."

JESUS COMES TO THE HILLS

Simon wondered if he was to go to work with his father the next day; but his mother said she wanted him to stay and help her. So his father set off alone, and Simon stayed at home to help.

"I want you to go to borrow some oil from James's mother," said Simon's mother, later on in the morning. "Don't stop and play with James. Come straight back."

Simon sped off. It was another lovely spring day, and the boy ran fast over the flower-spread grass. He came to James's, and asked for the oil. James was there and said he would walk back with him. The boys stood for a moment looking down at the lake. Then Simon noticed something.

"Look at all those people!" he said in wonder. "Look, James—do you see them? Crowding over the hillside as far as you can see! Whatever are they coming up into the hills for?"

James stared at the distant hillside, up which hundreds of people were streaming. "They're all coming from Capernaum, I should think," he said. "How queer! What can be happening? Mother! Come and look! What are all these people coming up into the hills for? Look, they are making their way round the head of the lake—hundreds of them." His mother gazed in wonder.

"Run and see what is happening," she said. The boys rushed off eagerly. They came at last to a group of four or five people. A woman called to them.

"You boys! Have you seen him? Is he anywhere near here?"

"Who? Who?" asked Simon and James, surprised.

"Have you seen him?"

"Jesus. We've come to find him. Look, do you see my poor little girl? She is so ill and no doctor can heal her. But Jesus can. We must find him."

The boys looked at the thin, pale child in the woman's arms. Her bones showed through her skin. "I haven't seen anyone strange here," said Simon, and he suddenly began to feel excited. "How do you know that this man is anywhere near here?"

"Somebody saw him get into a boat at Capernaum, with the men who follow him, his friends," said the woman. "He sailed away across the water. We think he will land somewhere here, and we have come to find him. Look at all the people who want to hear him!"

They all wanted Jesus. Where was he?

The boys gazed at all the crowds that were coming up the hillside. Some of the people were ill and in pain, but they were certain that if only they could find Jesus they would be better at once. Sometimes friends carried an ill man or woman between them. Mothers carried sick children. They all wanted one man —Jesus. Where was he?

Many people were as strong and well as Simon himself. They had come to hear Jesus talk. They wanted to see him do his miracles. He was so good, so powerful, so kind. Surely he must be the greatest man in the world! But where was he?

Nobody knew. The boat into which Jesus had stepped had sailed away to some secret place by the lake. Jesus was tired, and so were his disciples, the men who followed him and were his friends. They wanted to rest and be quiet in some peaceful spot up in the hills, far away from the busy town of Capernaum.

Peter, in whose boat Jesus went, knew

the country-side well at the other end of the lake. He knew the wild, quiet places, where Jesus might rest. Peter had been born there, at Bethsaida, and he was glad to take Jesus in his boat to the parts he knew so well as a boy.

The boat put in quietly at a little creek. Peter jumped out and made it fast. Jesus and the others stepped out and made their way up the quiet hillside.

"This is what we need," said Jesus. "Here, in this green, quiet place, we will talk and rest together. No one will disturb us here."

Soon, up in the quiet hills, the little company was at rest on the grass. Some fell asleep. Some lay down and watched the tiny clouds sail across the blue sky.

Some talked quietly. Peter kept near his master, glad to be alone with him at last. There had been so many people around him for so long. Now at last Jesus could rest.

But not far away were the great crowds that were seeking for Jesus. More and more men and women came to where the two boys, Simon and James, stood together.

"Do these boys know where he is?" said the men and women. Then someone gave a cry.

"We've seen the boat! Jesus and his disciples must have left it down below on the water and have gone up the hillside yonder. Surely those are men sitting on the grass, over on the next hill?"

But Jesus did not want to go away

The great crowds moved away at once towards the hillside where Jesus sat. Jesus saw them coming, and so did his disciples. Peter looked at his master in disappointment. Now the day would be full of work for Jesus. Was there time to get away before the crowds rushed upon them?

But Jesus did not want to go away. "They are like sheep without a shepherd," he said, full of pity for all the people coming towards him.

Simon and James were almost knocked over by the great crowds that pressed past them, to go to the next hillside to see Jesus.

"Shall we go too?" said Simon, in excitement.

"I'll go and ask my mother," said James. "You take your oil home and ask too."

The boys raced back to their homes. Simon burst in, panting. "Mother! Oh, Mother, that wonderful man Jesus has come near here in the hills. Can I go and see him? Mother, there are thousands of people out there! They have walked all the way from Capernaum!"

"Take me too," said Ruth at once.

"You're too little," said Simon. "You'd be frightened of the crowds. I've never seen so many people in my life. Oh, Mother, do say I may go for the rest of the day! Maybe Jesus will heal the sick people—and tell stories. May I go?"

"Yes, you may go," said his mother, smiling at Simon's hot, eager face. "You worked so well yesterday, you deserve a holiday. Come back this evening, and tell me all about it."

"Oh, thank you, Mother!" shouted Simon, and he rushed off at once. But his mother called him back.

"Simon! You can't go off without taking something to eat. Wait a minute now."

"Oh, I can't wait," shouted Simon, but he came back all the same, ready to snatch what his mother was preparing for him.

"Now look—here are five loaves for you," said his mother, putting the thick slices of bread into a basket. "And see—

here are the two little fishes you caught yesterday. I have pickled them for you and you can eat them with your bread."

"Oh, Mother, thank you! I shall like to eat the fishes I caught myself," said Simon. He took the basket with the five loaves and two fishes and rushed off excitedly. Perhaps he would see Jesus, and get close enough to him to hear a story. Perhaps he would see him lay his healing hands on a poor sick man or woman, or a weeping child, and make them better.

He forgot about James. He only thought of joining the crowds and looking for Jesus. He sped down the hill as fast as he could, and at last came to where the crowds were still pressing on and on.

"Now perhaps I shall see him!" thought the boy. "What will he look like? I shan't dare to speak to him—but I shall get as close to him as I can."

A WONDERFUL DAY

Jesus was there, in the midst of the great crowds. His disciples were trying to keep the people in order, so that they would not press too close. Those who had brought sick friends were taken to Jesus. Mothers with ill children begged to get closer. Everyone was excited.

"Is he there? Has he done anything wonderful yet? Oh, look at that mother! She is weeping, but she looks so happy!"

A little woman came pushing through the crowds, carrying a dark-eyed baby. "See!" she said, with the tears streaming down her cheeks. "He has touched my poor child and now she is better! She has been ill for months. Just a touch from his wonderful hand, and the colour came back to my baby's cheeks, and she smiled."

The crowd looked in silence at the happy mother, whose tears of joy fell all the time. The child crowed and reached out her hand. The mother pressed her close.

"A man like that should be king of all the world!" she said. "So kind, so good —he is indeed the Son of God!"

Simon saw the baby and the mother. He saw other people too, who had been healed by Jesus.

"I was a cripple, but he made my legs straight," shouted a man, coming

44

through the crowd. "See, I can walk again!"

Simon listened and stared. He saw a girl who had been blind, and she came joyfully by, looking wonderingly at everything. "She was blind!" said her mother, who was holding her by the arm. "Yes, blind since she was a baby. But Jesus put his fingers on her eyes and spoke to her. And she could see! Now this is the gladdest day of my life!"

Simon tried to push through the crowds. He wanted to get nearer to Jesus. He could not even guess where he was, because he was small and could not see over anyone's shoulder. The men did not like Simon's trying to push through, and they were rough with him.

The disciples came round among the people, talking to them, answering questions, and teaching them. Simon saw one of them, but did not dare to speak to him. If only he could go up to him and say, "Please will you take me to Jesus—just for a minute!"

Then word went round among the crowds. "He is going to talk. Jesus is going to tell us stories. We must be silent."

A great quiet fell on the crowds around Simon, and he heard a voice speaking. Every word fell clearly on the air. Simon listened, his heart beating. He couldn't see Jesus—but he could hear him.

It was a strong and lovely voice to

Jesus chose simple words, and told them stories

listen to, a warm, friendly voice that
spoke simply and clearly. The people
around Simon were poor simple folk,
who could not understand long words
and difficult teaching. So Jesus chose
simple words, and told them stories into
which he put the truths he wanted them
to learn: love one another—be honest—

be truthful—be just and generous to one another.

Simon listened; but he wanted to see as well as to hear. So he edged his way a little nearer. And then he saw Jesus.

He saw a man sitting on a rock. His head was bare to the sun. He had a face that Simon wanted to look at all day— a kind, strong face whose eyes could be filled with pity or could be dark and stern. Now they were filled with kindness and they looked from one to another of the crowd, as Jesus told his story.

Then Simon felt what many other people felt. His heart was swept with love and admiration for this amazing man, whose whole life was spent in helping others, and in bringing health and happiness to both bodies and souls.

"I wish I could do something for him," the boy said to himself. "If only I could! I should like to give him all I've got—but I've nothing he would like."

Simon stood and listened. He had no idea of the time at all. The sun had risen high up into the sky. Now it was going down again. It went lower and lower. The day was going.

The boy had not eaten anything all day. He had not felt hungry as he usually did—or if he had, he had not even noticed it. He had not once thought of his basket of food. He had only wanted to see and hear Jesus.

Simon saw some of the disciples go up

to Jesus and speak to him. "Master," they said, "this is a desert place, and the day is almost gone. Send the crowds away so that they may go into the country round about, and into the villages, and buy themselves bread, for they have nothing to eat."

And Jesus said, "Give them food to eat."

The disciples looked at their master. "Shall we then go and buy two hundred pennyworth of bread?" they said. "Shall we give a little to every man to eat?"

Simon edged a little nearer. People whispered around him. "Jesus says we must have something to eat. We are hungry. We have been here all day.

But where can we get food in such a place as this?"

Then Simon heard the clear voice of Jesus. "How many loaves have you? Go and see."

The disciples went about the crowd to see if anyone had brought bread. But either the people had forgotten to bring food in their excitement or it had been eaten long before. There seemed to be none.

Simon saw Andrew, one of the disciples, coming near, asking if anyone had any bread, and a sudden thought came into his head, and made his heart beat.

"I've my five loaves and two small fishes! I can give them to Jesus. Perhaps he will eat them himself. I wanted so badly to give him something—and perhaps I can." Simon went red and his eyes shone. Andrew came nearer.

"Has anyone any bread?"

Simon pushed his way nearer to Andrew. The disciple felt a touch on his arm, and turned. A small boy was standing by him, holding up a basket with five loaves and two rather small fishes.

"You can have mine," said Simon, his face redder than ever. "Will they do?"

Andrew nodded, smiling. He led Simon right up to Jesus, and the boy looked into that kind, strong face, and saw the dark and friendly eyes. Simon could not say a word.

"There is a lad here who has five barley loaves and two small fishes," said

"You can have mine," said Simon

Andrew. "But what are they among so many?"

Jesus looked at the slices of bread and the little pickled fish. Then he looked at the great crowds on the hillside: one thousand—two, three, four, perhaps five thousand! And he had five barley loaves and two small fishes to feed so many.

"Make the people sit down in groups of fifty or a hundred," said Jesus. So the disciples went among the crowds, and made them sit down in orderly groups. Simon still stood beside Jesus, proud and happy.

What was Jesus going to do?

SIMON SEES A MIRACLE

Now the people were sitting quietly in companies together, waiting, their faces turned towards Jesus. The disciples came back to him.

Jesus took the loaves from Simon's basket and held them in his hands. Then he looked up to heaven and said grace, blessing the loaves in his hands. He broke them into pieces, and then he broke the fishes too.

Simon watched. With each piece of broken bread Jesus put a bit of the pickled fish. He handed them to the waiting disciples, and at once they began to go among the people to feed them.

Jesus went on breaking up the bread and the fish. Again and again the disciples came back to him and then went to the waiting crowds and gave them the food. More and more people were fed, dozens of them, hundreds of them —yes, thousands.

Simon watched in awe and amazement. How could his five loaves and two little fishes feed so many people? He had only brought enough for himself to eat during the day. But in Jesus' hands his basket of food became enough to feed these hungry thousands. It was a miracle!

"A miracle!" said Simon to himself, his eyes shining. "I have seen a miracle done with my own little loaves and fishes. Because he pitied the hungry

"Did you like the fish?" he asked

people, Jesus has taken my basket of food, and made it enough for us all. How glad I am I forgot to eat it!"

Everyone ate and there was enough

and to spare. Jesus and the disciples ate, too—and Simon ate with them. The bread and the fish tasted exactly the same as usual, although Simon thought they might taste different, because of the miracle.

Jesus turned and smiled at the proud little boy. Simon spoke to him shyly.

"Did you like the fish?" he asked. "I caught them myself. And my mother made the loaves."

"You must tell her what happened to them," said Jesus. "And now see—everyone has finished. Go round with my disciples and pick up the pieces."

Jesus did not like food to be wasted, and neither did he wish the lovely hill-side to be spoilt by so many scraps.

Simon went with the disciples to pick up all the pieces—and to his great amazement they filled twelve baskets!

"I brought only one small basket of food—but we have filled twelve with the crumbs!" he said to the disciples in wonder. "Truly your master is a wonderful man. If I were old enough I would follow him, too. I have seen how good and kind he is, and I wish I could be one of his disciples, like you."

Now the sun was very low. Jesus called the disciples to him.

"Go down into the boat," he said. "Do not wait for me. I will send away the people to their homes."

The disciples did not want to leave Jesus behind, but they obeyed his word.

They went down to the boat that rocked on the water far below.

Then Jesus sent the great crowds away. It would soon be dark and they had a long way to go. They had been fed, but they were tired and they must get home before the small children fell asleep on the way.

So Jesus said good-bye to them himself, and in little companies the people turned to go over the hills to their homes. They talked excitedly of all that had happened. What a wonderful man Jesus was! If only he could be their king! How they loved him and honoured him —surely never, never had there been such a man in the world before!

Talking in this way the crowds left the

quiet hillside. Simon stood watching them, wondering suddenly where James was. He had forgotten all about James. What had happened to him? Did he know about the loaves and the fishes?

A voice called to him. "Simon! Where were you all the day? When I saw you at last, you were with the disciples— you were quite near Jesus! How did you get so close?"

"James! Did you have some of the bread and the pickled fish?" said Simon, running to James and taking hold of his arm.

"Of course I did. Everybody did. I'd eaten all my food and I was very hungry."

"James, the bread and the fish you had

61

were the loaves my mother baked, and the two fish I caught with you yesterday!" said Simon. "I know you can't believe me—but it's true. Jesus took them and broke them and there was enough for everyone! It was one of his miracles. I saw him—it was *my* bread and fish!"

"Oh, Simon!" said James in amazement. "What will your mother say?"

"Let's go and tell her!" said Simon, excitement sweeping over him again. "Come quickly."

They darted off, leaving the empty hillside. Then Simon saw, not far away, walking steadily along the hill path that led to the high mountain, a figure that he never forgot all his life long.

It was Jesus.

Jesus was alone. He was tired. He wanted to pray to God, his Father. He was walking up to the high mountain, where he would pray for strength, and be near to God.

Simon pulled James back. "Look— there he is. You can almost see the goodness shining out of his face. We've seen the greatest man in the world, James. He must be going to the mountain to pray. Let us be quiet and go another way."

The boys ran off quietly, thinking of the silent figure they had seen, walking alone. Then they remembered the excitements of the long, sunny day, and Simon began to shout as they came near to his home, gleaming white in the falling twilight.

"Mother! Mother, are you there? I've had the most wonderful day of my life!"

Simon's mother looked up as the boy rushed in at the door, followed by James.

"Mother, Jesus did many miracles to-day—but do you know which was the biggest one he did? He took your bread and the two little fishes I caught—and he fed thousands of people with them."

"Tell me too," said Ruth. So Simon sat down and told his family again and again and again all that had happened that day. "I have seen Jesus," said Simon. "And I have seen a miracle. Surely nothing can ever happen to me more wonderful than this!"